Staying in the Helicopter®

Staying in the Helicopter®

The Key to Profitable Growth

secrets and tools to give big picture improvements in your sustained profitable growth

by Roger Harrop

LeHeup Limited

Anchor House

Cuxham Road

Watlington

OX49 5JW

United Kingdom

Tel: +44 1491 613635

Email: roger@rogerharrop.com

www.rogerharrop.com

skype: rogerharrop

Staying in the Helicopter
First published by LeHeup Ltd in 2005 (ISBN 0-9549586-0-8)
Revised edition published in 2006 by LeHeup Limited
Reprinted 2008, 2009
ISBN 0-9549586-1-6

British Library Cataloguing in Publication Data. A catalogue record
for this book is available from the British Library

Cover design by Rock Kitchen Harris
Book design by Word4Word Design & Publishing Ltd
Printed in the UK by TJ International, Padstow

Contents

Keynotes, Seminars, Workshops, Masterclasses and Strategic Retreats

Over 10,000 CEOs can't be wrong!

Roger Harrop is an international speaker who inspires and entertains his audiences with his acclaimed Staying in the Helicopter® series. Over 10,000 CEOs, business owners, managers and others have achieved transformational growth through his thought-provoking and entertaining speeches and workshops laced with real-life stories, anecdotes and humour. He is a former CEO of a highly successful high-tech, multinational, publicly quoted company, consultant, author, mentor and leadership tutor.

Roger's Highly Acclaimed Signature Programme

 'Staying in the Helicopter®' – the key to profitable growth in good times or bad.

For CEOs, MDOs, Business Audiences, Boards, Directors, Trustees, Senior Managers, whole company teams.

Staying in the Helicopter

Supplementary Programmes

 'Staying in the Helicopter®' - for sparkling sales in good times or bad

For CEOs, MDOs, Sales & Marketing Directors, VPs and Managers, whole sales teams.

 'Staying in the Helicopter®' - and building successful strategies

For CEOs, MDOs, Boards, Directors, Trustees

 'Staying in the Helicopter®' - and avoid change failing

For CEOs, MDOs, Boards, Directors, Trustees, Senior Managers

 'Staying in the Helicopter®' - the key to great leadership

For CEOs, MDOs, Business Audiences, Boards, Directors, Trustees, Senior Managers.

 'Staying in the Helicopter®' - with the right people

For CEOs, MDOs, Directors, Trustees, HR Directors, VPs and Managers.

Keynote Speeches, Seminars and Workshops

What People Say

Roger, you would undoubtedly be our Speaker of the Year

Brian Chernett, Chairman, The Academy for Chief Executives

Your workshop was very good and I can use a lot of your material directly in my work.

Dato' Dr Abdul Rahim Daud, Director, Telekom Malaysia Group Bhd

Fantastic - I feel like I've done an MBA in half a day!

Alex Robertson, Managing Director, HL Display Limited

I found your presentation, and I am sure I am speaking for a vast majority of those who attended the conference, one of the best in its genre I have witnessed - it was poignant, precise and engaging.

Viswa Sadisivan, Chairman, The Right Angle Group of Companies, Singapore

Staying in the Helicopter

Your speech was outstanding, and the way you interacted with my members was extremely effective. The content was awesome, and your delivery style was excellent

Joe D Adams, Group Chairman, The Academy for Chief Executives

'Experienced! Authentic! Articulate! Roger wowed the crowd in Singapore and it was a pleasure to work with a truly professional individual! '

Dave Rogers, Director, XL Results Foundation

Thank you so much for Staying in the Helicopter this afternoon. It was honestly the most thought-provoking two hours I have spent in my 35 years in business.

Stephen Hill, Consulting Alternatives

Thank for sharing your 'helicopter' concepts with our delegates. We received excellent feedback and they found the session very useful.

Patricia Enslow, Director Strategic Marketing, Citigroup Private Bank

What People Say

Author's Notes

For ease I have used 'CEO' throughout the book but its secrets, tools and lessons are relevant to everyone who is, or aspires to be, a leader in the organisation.

If you are reading this book then it is likely that you are running a business or are in some way involved in running a business. My experience of people like you is that you have little free time, that you don't like waffle and that you like to see ideas and initiatives translated into specific, quantifiable benefits to you and your business.

To that end you will find on page 64 a blank My Profitable Growth Matrix™ (PGM) for you to complete along with prompts as you journey through the book and discover the secrets and tools to bring you that sustained profitable growth you seek.

Over 10,000 CEOs, directors and managers have attended my Staying in the Helicopter® presentations and workshops and completed their own PGMs with universally dramatic results in terms of profitable growth. A typical PGM completed by a group of 12 experienced CEOs is shown on page 60.

10,000 CEOs can't be wrong!

Staying in the Helicopter®
The Key to Profitable Growth

Successful CEOs inevitably find themselves spending the greater part of their time dealing with the day-to-day.

When they do take time out they may invest in developing their own skills – and occasionally they may 'get up in the helicopter' to view the bigger picture.

In this book I demonstrate the benefits of more regularly taking the opportunity to step outside the day-to-day constraints of the business and focus on the wider horizon.

CEOs will, after reading this book, be stimulated to:

- *significantly improve the sustained profitable growth of their business*

- *improve their own effectiveness*

- *reduce their own levels of stress*

- *develop those under them.*

Specialists, experts, consultants and gurus seem to delight in generating complexity and jargon. My belief is that business is essentially simple and the successful CEO cuts through 'business speak' to the simple truths at the core.

In this book I have combined my personal experience with key pieces of research and business models to bring to the CEO simple, profound and valuable practical tools for immediate use.

I provide a specific, easy to use and relevant check list that helps the CEO do what probably nobody else can in their business - stay in the helicopter!

The Real Objective

So where do we start looking from our helicopter? As Stephen Covey put it in his book *The 7 Habits of Highly Effective People*:

...begin with the end in mind

There is only one place to start – the business purpose. I come across many businesses, however, that seem to subscribe to the Christopher Columbus school of management:

- *He left but he didn't know where he was going*

- *When he got there he didn't know where he was*

- *When he got back he didn't know where he had been*

- *....and he did this three times in seven years!*

What is your business purpose – the Real Objective?

More enlightened CEOs will, of course, have spent time thinking about and developing business company mission statements and objectives, but you must ask yourself:

Have I flown high enough in my helicopter?

Have I flown high enough in my helicopter?

I used to run a publicly quoted company and for them, you might think, the real objective is obvious and consistent – 'shareholder value' - and here's a former Chairman of Coca-Cola in their annual report saying just that:

> ... *our publicly stated mission is to create value over time for the owners of our business. In fact, in our society, that is the mission of any business: to create value for its owners.*

> **Robert C. Goizueta**

However, here is another public company chairman with quite a different view:

> ... I have always said that our management values jobs before profits. Lately, I've become surer than ever that this thinking is correct. We don't give a hoot about things like return on equity.

Ken Aikawa, Chairman, Mitsubishi Heavy Industries

Privately owned businesses can be more complex. The original reasons for setting up the business may have been lost or changed over time, and new generations may have taken over. Often, I find the real purpose of the business has never been discussed and it takes an outside independent advisor or director - who can be wholly unbiased and objective - to ask open questions of the owners and directors to tease out and agree precisely what the real purpose of the business is today.

Why is this important? Well, quite simply, if you don't know where you are trying to get to then it's unlikely that you are going to get there!

A *fundamentally* different strategy and approach is demanded to successfully run a business for shareholder value, rather than to preserve jobs, or for cash generation, or to minimise profits or to maximise the sale value of the business.

On this last point I always ask the same initial question of private business owners:

> *'Is your intention to ultimately hand the business on to successors or to sell it?'*

Frequently I get the reply:

> *'Well, if I get a good offer then I'd certainly sell.'*

It simply isn't like this: if you wish to sell your business for the highest possible price then you must spend three to five years running the business in a totally different way to how you have before.

Is our overriding business purpose crystal clear?

So – define your purpose. Get it to one sentence, then to half a sentence. Then focus on it like a laser beam - and you will then stand a very good chance of getting there!

Discipline of Market Leaders

Having clearly established the purpose of the business you then need to be clear about the 'shape' of the business and set a market leading strategy. Is it worth setting your sights any lower?

Have we set a market leading strategy?

Treacy and Wiersma extensively researched market leading companies across a wide range of market sectors worldwide – from SMEs to multinational corporations.

Their conclusions are fundamentally simple: market leaders need to be leaders in one of three basic disciplines:

- *Operational Excellence*

- *Product Leadership*

- *Customer Intimacy*

They must aim to be leader in one - but just one - and they need to be at least 'industry average' in all three. If they are not they are likely to have a weakness that undermines their strengths in other areas.

Operational Excellence

The essence – to be the lowest cost provider in the market:

- *Optimised supply chain processes*

- *Standardised, simplified, tightly controlled operations and decision systems*

- *Customers receive reliable high speed transactions*

- *'Lean and mean' culture where operational efficiency is highly rewarded*

- *Approaches to continuous improvement are deeply ingrained*

What businesses do I know who fit this model?

Product Leadership

The essence - to push the boundaries of the market with innovative products:

- *Focus on invention, product development and market exploitation*

- *Products and services generate anticipation and excitement among customers*

- *Adaptable structures that encourage entrepreneurism*

- *Rewards for new product successes and toleration of failures*

- *Seek to create new markets by going beyond currently articulated needs*

What businesses do I know who fit this model?

Customer Intimacy

The essence - to develop the relationship with your chosen customers that they most value:

What businesses do I know who fit this model?

- Focus on identifying customer problems and developing and implementing solutions

- Empowered customer-facing employees

- Carefully selected and nurtured clients

- Specific solution culture thriving on dedicated repeat customers

What does the hearbeat of my organisation say about where the focus and energy is?

- Organisational versatility to customise products and services

Whichever discipline you choose to excel in, what you should always strive to do, as Michel Robert puts it, is:

Staying in the Helicopter

8

Get your competitors to play in your sandbox, not theirs

In other words your offer needs to be innovative – and if possible change the rules of the whole game. Amazon.com and SpecSavers are great examples of organisations that did just this.

I suggest you regularly get together your six or eight most lateral and 'out-of-the-box' thinkers in the organisation – never mind what jobs they have – and put them in a room for a couple of hours, with no interruptions, and plenty of flip charts. Encourage them to think about your business from first principles and to challenge the paradigms about the business, products, processes, markets, sectors, routes to market – indeed every aspect of what you do and why.

Do we have mechanisms in place to generate ideas for 'new sandboxes'.

I *guarantee* that sooner or later from those sessions you will get a gold nugget of an idea that might just force your competitors to have to come and play in your sandbox.

Complete the two grids on page 10 with the 'shape' of your business today and your target for tomorrow – and then share it with the whole company.

Discipline of Market Leaders

What shape are we now?

	Customer Intimacy	Product & Process Innovation	Operational Excellence
Market Leader			
Fast Follower			
Industry Average			
Below industry average			

What shape is our target?

	Customer Intimacy	Product & Process Innovation	Operational Excellence
Market Leader			
Fast Follower			
Industry Average			
Below industry average			

Real Business Control

Where next in our helicopter? – well now we need to get into some left brain stuff.

To run your business effectively it is essential that you have the right financial and other key performance indicators provided to you. You need to remember, however, that (regardless of what others may think) this information is there simply to help you run the business.

You must, therefore, ensure that you get it in a format, in a level of detail and using terminology that you are happy with.

Accountants, just like most professions, make their activities appear more complex and difficult to understand than necessary. I think it must be some form of self-preservation activity that we all have!

So let's start with the terminology:

Each of these terms means exactly the same thing:

- *orders = bookings*
- *order book = backlog*
- *backlog = overdue orders = back orders (sometimes)*
- *sales = revenues = turnover*
- *cost of goods sold = cost of sales*
- *gross profit = trading profit = contribution*
- *operating profit = trading profit = PBIT = EBIT = surplus = EBITDA (sometimes)*
- *earnings (sometimes) = EBT = PBT = net profit*
- *debtors = receivables*

Staying in the Helicopter

- *creditors = payables*

- *stock = inventory (sometimes)*

- *cash = liquidity*

- *work in progress = work in process*

And there are many more *(see *note)*.

You need to get in your helicopter and take control – you're the boss. Decide which accounting terminology (company finance-speak) you wish to adopt and then make everyone, including your auditors, stick with that in everything you, and they, do.

Take control of your company finance-speak

---

* *When writing this chapter I put this list to about a dozen financial people around the world. I received back some very pedantic statements that I was wrong and that certain terms were definitely not equivalent and had quite different meanings. The problem was, however, not all of these pedantic statements agreed with each other!*

Real Business Control

So, having got your terminology fixed the next thing you need to be clear about is the information you need and the way in which you want it to be presented.

All the figures you see in a set of accounts are, by definition, historical, but what you need to do to run the business effectively is look to the future. Running a business successfully is much more about looking at trends rather than absolute figures and you need to track key financial, and other information month on month, year on year and against budget to really see the direction the business is going in.

Look at financial trends more than absolute numbers

It is so easy to get bogged down in the detailed numbers and miss the big picture – and I've actually seen this more with large Corporates than with SMEs.

I worked for Burmah Oil at one time and their monthly reporting packs and annual budget papers were up to 50 pages long! They were not drawn up in any way to help the CEO run the business. When I was at BTR, however, the reverse was true. They had the most outstanding monthly reporting pack I have come across – it was never more than ten pages and the first page summary gave you an instant overview of the business from which you could then drill down as necessary into any areas of concern. I've since used that format in many companies and if you'd like a copy just drop me an email at roger@rogerharrop.com

So what information do you need on this all important summary sheet?

- *Start with what's most important to you - **Profit** (assuming your purpose in some way embraces profitable growth)*

- *If you're in the type of business where there is a time lag between receiving the order and making the sale, then next you need **Order Input** as this is the very first indication you get of what's going on in the business.*

- *Also have **Order Book** so you can see what you've got to go at.*

- ***ROS** (Return on Sales) – see later*

- Depending on the business, one or two **Balance Sheet Items** always including **Receivables**.

- **Cash Flow** is very important

- **People Numbers**

- One or two Non-Financial Ratios which are relevant to your business, for example OTIF (delivery on time in full) and maybe a quality, customer satisfaction, service level or a health and safety measure.

Have a simple front summary sheet to your monthly pack

The above information alone shown month on month, tracked against last year and your budget should give you sufficient trend indications to see instantly the health of the business and how things are going.

Next, I have always found the need to get in the helicopter and look at the big picture. This is more important with financial information than probably any other area of the business, because it's so easy to get drawn into the detailed numbers.

Staying in the Helicopter

Whenever you are comparing year on year, or looking a year or two ahead, I would recommend that you draw up a simple 'helicopter' P&L account with *only* those 7 elements shown below. In the Corporate environment I've found this particularly valuable, for example, when you are reviewing a budget a subsidiary company has put forward to you for approval:

- *Orders*

- *Sales*

- *Materials or costs (excluding all labour)*

- *Payroll & associated costs*

- *Depreciation*

- *All other overheads*

- *PBIT*

Prepare a very simple P&L when comparing or forecasting

If you're in a manufacturing business then as likely as not you will have some element of labour and factory overhead taken into your product costing and your gross margin calculation. I find whenever comparing year on year this can really make true comparisons difficult. So, if you have such a business you will need to have a further line included above of labour, overhead and

'000s	Full Year			
	Actual This Year		Budget This Year	
Orders	5150		6600	
Sales	4500		5750	
Materials	1845	41.0%	2358	41.0%
Payroll	720	16.0%	1092	19.0%
Depreciation	180	4.0%	250	4.3%
Other Overheads	1080	24.0%	1300	22.6%
Operating Profit	675		750	
ROS	15.0%		13.0%	

materials going into or coming out of stock (just one figure) and then ensure all people costs are in the payroll line to complete the P&L statement.

If your purpose, like many businesses, embraces sustained profitable growth then a key performance indicator is ROS (Return On Sales), which is operating profit as a percentage of sales. What you are seeking to ensure is that not only your absolute profit figure increases year on year but also that your ROS improves every single year.

Seek to improve your ROS every year

For that to happen, of course, one or more of the P&L elements below the sales level in the P&L must be reducing as a percentage of sales.

The key ratios you should therefore look at in the above P&L when comparing, say, a budget for next year with forecast performance for the current year are simply the individual line ratios against sales - because only by each of those reducing can the ROS increase. It really is that simple!

In the example on the left, on first sight, the budget for next year looks reasonable with the profit improving by over 10%. However when you look at the ROS it is budgeted to go down by two percentage points – not good. On inspection we can see that whilst the margin has been maintained and the Other Overhead ratio has gone down – as it should with increased sales volume – there is a significant increase in payroll costs budgeted. Why? Is there a plan to pay big bonuses or take on additional people – or what?

We've concentrated so far mainly on the P&L but, of course, businesses go bust because of a lack of cash not a lack of profit.

Control of working capital (essentially receivables, payables and inventory) is very important for you to monitor.

Do cash flow forecasts regularly

You should regularly look at receivables days and inventory days (where appropriate) and have a discipline of doing regular cash flow forecasting, which really isn't hard to do with a reasonable degree of accuracy no matter what your business is.

Finally in this section I'd like to touch on budgeting for sustained profitable growth.

I have seen, and indeed prepared, many budgets over the years and nine times out of ten growth budgets are predicated on one assumption only and that is that sales volumes are going to increase, which will in turn generate improved profits.

This is not a robust budget and is very likely to be missed – and missed badly since what you often find is that the overheads and people numbers have been allowed to increase on the back of the predicted sales growth and when that growth doesn't happen there is in fact a 'double whammy' hit on profitability.

I was taught a great 'helicopter' discipline by BTR:

> In order for a budget to be robust it needs to represent a three-legged stool.

Make sure your budget is robust

What this means is that the budgeted profit improvement should come from three areas equally (or the stool falls over!).

They are:

- *sales volume*

- *price increases & cost reductions (margin improvement)*

- *productivity.*

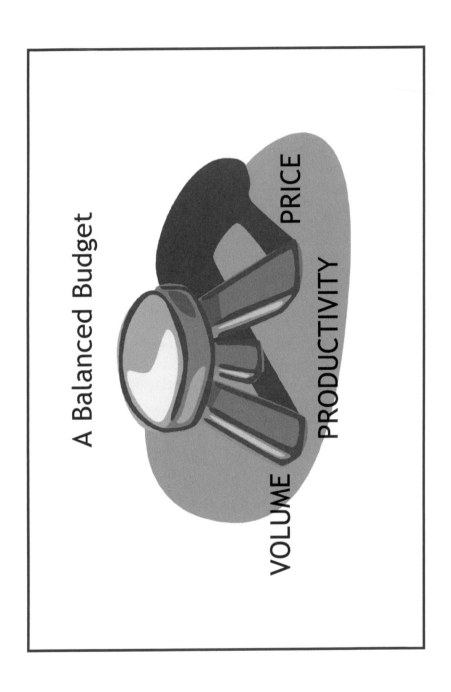

A Balanced Budget

VOLUME

PRODUCTIVITY

PRICE

22

So in your budget you should quantify clearly the profit impact of each and work on getting that impact about equal.

The simplest and most useful way of measuring productivity, incidentally, is just sales divided by total people numbers. Don't bother with all the more complex or sophisticated productivity measures, they simply aren't necessary.

There we are then - a full set of 'helicopter' figures that should work for you to achieve your business purpose.

I can now hear you saying to yourself that it's all very interesting but you can really rely on your accountant, finance director or controller (depending upon the size of your business) to do all this analysis and monitoring for you and you should not need to worry about it.

Don't leave the numbers to the accountants!

Please do not make that assumption - it's very dangerous.

It's your job to run the business, and that means that it's your job to keep a grip on the key numbers and trends.

Reasons Why Customers Leave

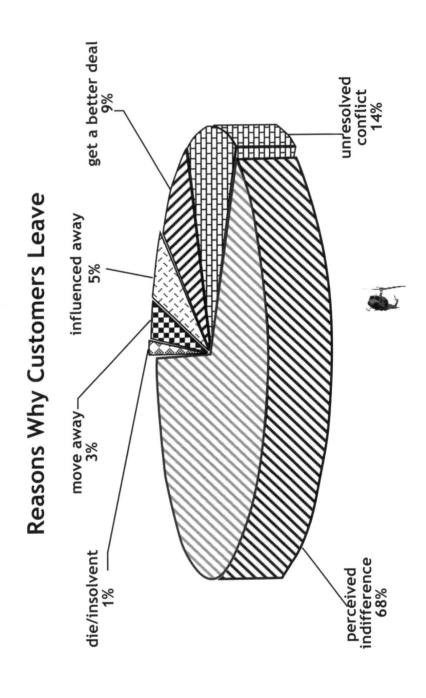

Profitable Growth

The operational target of most businesses is that all elusive profitable growth.

Assuming margins and costs are under control then it is reasonable to assume that profitable growth is principally dependant upon sales growth. The result of this is that I often find that a tremendous focus is placed on, and significant investment made into, the generation of new customers above all else.

Why? Why? Why?

when there are other ways to increase sales and profits each involving less risk, less investment and with more likelihood of success?

Why look for new customers first?

Let's start with lost customers.

Michael LeBoeuf refers to some interesting results of extensive research across companies big and small as to why customers go elsewhere. See page 24 for an illustration.

Here is a first opportunity to avoid spending vast sums chasing new customers!

If you can address the 82% who leave because of unresolved conflict and perceived indifference and aim to win a good percentage back, your growth targets must become easier to achieve. Then, of course, you need to put in place the mechanisms to ensure that you won't lose them, or indeed other customers, again.

The best antidote to perceived indifference is regular and varied communication at all levels. Classic wisdom is that your clients and prospective clients need to hear from you at least once every six weeks if they are not to consider that you don't care about them.

When did you, or your business, last say thank you to your customers?

Do you share your long term strategy with your customers?

Say 'thank you' to your customers

Do you involve them in your new product development?

When did you last invite their CEO to dinner? When you were *not* after something specific?

Overall, of course, you need to strive for the achievement of outstanding levels of service to your customers if they are to remain loyal and even better, become advocates of you – a free sales force. You need to address not only your products but also your delivery processes – how many times have you clicked the 'contact us' button on a website and made an enquiry only to receive no response – ever!

How do we regain and retain lost customers?

Have a think, then, about how you not only get back those customers you have lost due to unresolved conflict and perceived indifference but also how you ensure they don't go for these reasons in the future. In my Helicopter workshops it is quite normal for delegates to come up with 15-20 specific initiatives to do just this.

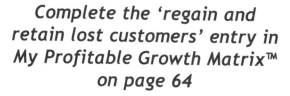

Complete the 'regain and retain lost customers' entry in My Profitable Growth Matrix™ on page 64

We have now worked on regaining lost customers and on retaining those we have. Next, do we need to embark on finding new customers to get the growth we seek? The answer is still NO!

Let's look next at existing customers.

I suggest you target and measure three metrics – ones that you will rarely find in any set of accounts or management information pack, but which are very easy

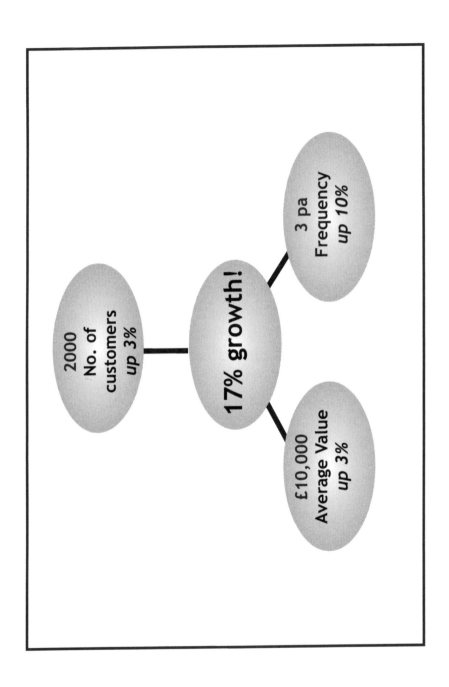

28

to establish for any business:

- *Number of customers*
- *Average order value*
- *Frequency of order placement*

By setting and achieving modest growth targets for all three you will readily achieve your overall sales growth aspirations.

Don't believe me? Try this.

Let's say you have 2000 customers, that they each, on average buy three times per annum and their average order value is £10,000. Let's then set really modest growth targets – say, 3% more customers, order value up 3% and frequency up to 3.3 per annum. Do the maths... that alone gives sales growth of 17% !!

This growth is principally dependent on the development of your existing customers – and it is much easier to work with them than to go out, find and secure business from new customers.

How do we increase revenue from existing customers?

Complete the 'increase order
value and frequency' entry in
My Profitable Growth Matrix™
on page 64

Finally in our search for 'free' profitable growth we cannot ignore price.

I worry that some companies have, on the one hand, forgotten how to increase prices and, on the other, are pre-disposed to respond favourably to requests for discounts - 'to get volume' or for other reasons.

Faced with these requests, I urge CEOs in their helicopter to just keep the maths in front of them:

For a business with, for example, a 30% gross margin:

Do I think
twice before
reducing
prices?

- If you reduce prices by 10%
  and wish to maintain the
  same profit level you need
  a resulting 50% increase in
  volume - just to stand still.
  In reality, of course, for
  such a large volume
  increase you would
  probably require increases

Staying in the Helicopter

30

in fixed overhead,
premium time working,
etc. demanding an even
greater volume increase to
stand still

■ *If you increase prices by*
10% however, the maths
show that you can afford
to lose 25% of your
customers and still
maintain profit levels

Ask yourself - what would truly be the effect of increasing your prices by, say, 1% - today?

Can we increase our prices TODAY?

Complete the 'price' entry in
My Profitable Growth Matrix™
on page 64

So, having first spent time developing and retaining your existing customers you do finally have to consider the ways to go about seeking and securing new customers.

CEOs will have all kinds of proposals placed in front of them to achieve this aim – advertising, exhibitions, discounts, new sales literature, additional salespeople, new distributors, websites etc., etc.

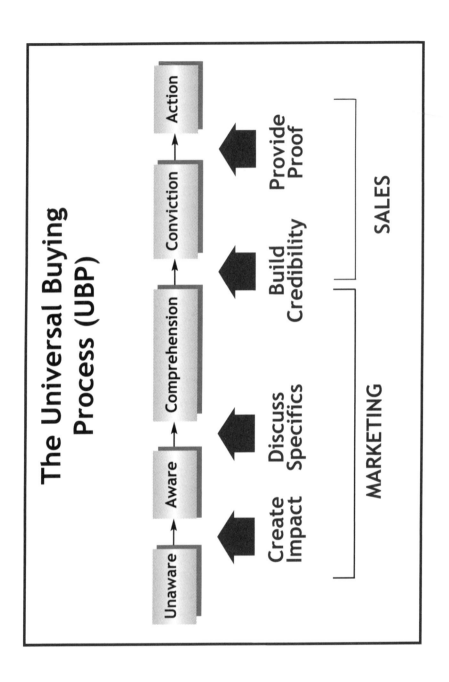

The Universal Buying Process (UBP)

Unaware → Aware → Comprehension → Conviction → Action

Create Impact

Discuss Specifics

Build Credibility

Provide Proof

MARKETING

SALES

The customer-facing professions, marketing and sales (of which I am a member!) seem to love to indulge in buzz words, acronyms, jargon and often the most complex of business models.

You need to cut through all this, to 'keep it simple' and then ask the important, customer-related questions.

Each and every time you review such proposals I would encourage you to view them from your helicopter in the context of the Universal Buying Process (see page 32).

Do we have mechanisms in place to address each stage in the UBP?

This is simply that process we all have to go through every time we either buy or sell something. Whatever the proposition, CEOs should ask:

> *What are we trying to do, and at what point are we in the Universal Buying Process?*

Profitable Growth

CEOs should then:

- *Evaluate whether that is what the business needs and whether the specific proposal in front of them is targeted to that aim*

- *And ensure that there are specific processes in place to take potential customers through each step in the process*

In thinking about a promotional programme of any kind I would urge you to 'think outside the box' – the most successful campaigns are the most innovative and creative – and they do not need to be expensive.

For example 'viral marketing' techniques – essentially having your message transmitted throughout the internet by amused recipients – have developed over recent years and can be extremely cheap and have dramatic results:

Is all our marketing truly creative?

The amusing clip shown on page 36 (see also www.theviralfactory.com) was inexpensive to produce and was sent initially to 5 people. The next day one person visited the website advertised, the day after that 9, by the 23rd day 13,588 visited.

In the first month the site had 233,652 unique visitors and at the time of writing it is claimed that in excess of 25 million have seen the clip.

You must agree that this is a highly cost-effective promotion by any standards!

Having addressed the marketing side of the equation it's worth reminding ourselves from our helicopter of the recognised truths that apply to successful selling:

- *Everyone in the business that ever has any kind of contact with customers needs to be a salesperson and trained as such*

- *The very best salespeople spend 90% of their time on the customer relationship, and only 10% on trying to sell them something*

Is our sales and marketing activity smart and simple rather than complex and expensive?

Successful selling depends most on the enthusiasm and belief exhibited by the salesperson and much less on sales skills and product knowledge than we often imagine.

Profitable Growth

Headrush – intentionally viral

> ## Complete the 'helicopter sales and marketing' entry in My Profitable Growth Matrix™ on page 64

Finally in this section - as you wind down at the end of the week and look down from your helicopter - have a think about

Why should I buy from us?

Why should I buy from us?

Have a look at the whole process of contact with clients from the very first contact through to the last and see how easy you make it for them to buy from you - and how attractive. Put out on a table an example of every customer-facing communication or material you have - you will be shocked the first time you do it!

Team Performance

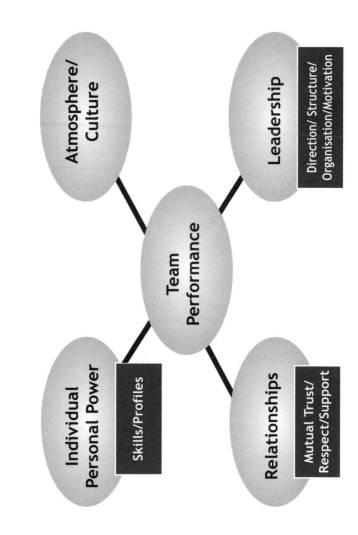

People

People, and the leadership of people, are at the very core of every organisation and here too effective leaders need to look at themselves, and their teams, from the helicopter.

Team performance comes from four key areas (see the diagram on page 38).

How often, for example, do we see football teams full of 'stars' with all the technical ability in the world but which are not successful?

There may be many reasons for this but it is likely that a whole dimension of team selection has not been considered. When recruiting we all look at 'technical' ability, 'chemistry' and maybe some psychometric and other results, but the individual's pre-disposed psychological team profile is also vital to developing a truly high-performing team (a very exciting place to be incidentally!)

In this area I find Belbin's Team Roles model (see page 40) to be one of the most practical and useful of the various tools available and it often rapidly becomes assimilated into the culture of the business.

Belbin's Team Roles

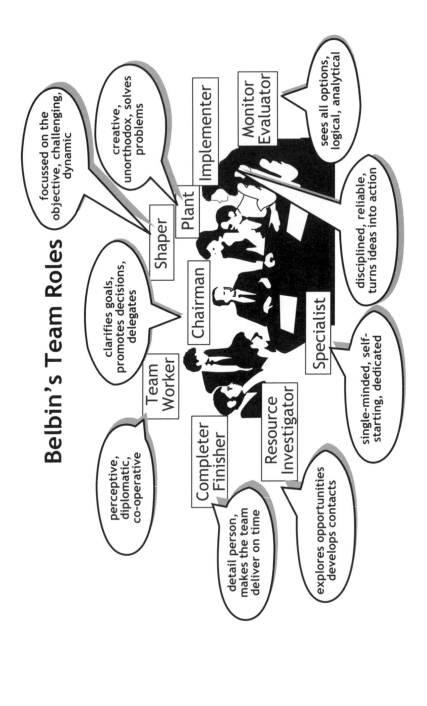

40

An effective team does not, of course, have to include every role, but from my direct observation as a tutor of disparate delegate teams attending a leading experiential leadership programme over 20 years, it is certainly true that a performing team must at least include one person from each of the four quadrants of the task execution model on page 42.

Something else that is often overlooked is the importance of recognising that in the execution of a task or project different Team Roles become important at different stages in the process.

Do we have an adequate mix of Belbin team profiles in each of our teams?

Complete the 'Belbin selected teams' entry in My Profitable Growth Matrix™ on page 64

People

Task Execution

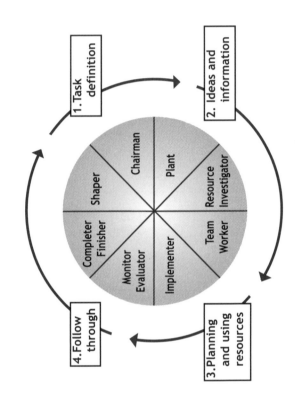

1. Task definition

2. Ideas and information

3. Planning and using resources

4. Follow through

Chairman

Shaper

Plant

Resource Investigator

Completer Finisher

Monitor Evaluator

Implementer

Team Worker

Get the Right Person

NO - don't skip this section!

I deliberately didn't call it 'recruiting' as I knew you probably wouldn't read it if I did!

I recently surveyed Business Leaders of large companies and small, profit and not-for-profit, and I asked just them just one question:

> *'What is the single biggest factor that you believe will inhibit your sustained profitable growth into the future?'*

Close to 40% responded that it was people - the recruitment, motivation and retention of people that will be the biggest factor.

So, firstly, recruitment has got to be worth putting some effort into if you are going to achieve that sustained profitable growth you seek.

> *OK - hands up everyone who uses just one or two interviews to recruit people.*

> *Well if you do let me say now that YOU ARE CRAZY!*

But you're in good company. I am amazed at just how many companies around the world from the very smallest to the very largest still just use one or two interviews to recruit people and then talk about 'chemistry' being a main factor in selecting a candidate.

Statistically the success rate you will achieve using this method is just two in five.

THAT'S A 60% FAILURE RATE!

'Traditional' recruiting methods give a 60% failure rate

Is there anywhere else in your businesses where you would accept that degree of failure?

There are proven methodologies that I use that will move your success rate up to maybe four out of every five being recruitment successes.

Isn't that worth investing some time in ?

Unfortunately, I do believe the answer seems to be 'no' for a lot of Business Leaders and managers - simply because it is they who have to work at it and they who have to invest their precious time – and other priorities intrude.

I believe it is worth it – it's massively worth it – and indeed, from where I sit in my

Staying in the Helicopter

helicopter I see it as a vital part of your job to ensure that you get the right people for the right jobs throughout your organisation.

We need to be much more sophisticated in our recruiting methodology.

There are comprehensive methodologies that will dramatically improve your recruiting success rate. They, of course, take longer and cost more, but this is nothing compared with the cost of getting it wrong. I saw some figures recently that estimated that the total cost to the organisation of recruiting the wrong person to be around five times the individual's annual salary!

I see recruiting as a four stage process with each stage being of equal importance.

Always write a job and person specification

To start you need to be clear about what you want - the specification of the job and the specification of the person that you are looking for to fill it – and please don't delegate it to the HR department or your PA to do!

This may appear painfully obvious but so often I find this has not been done, certainly not written down, and the thought seems to be 'we'll decide when we see who comes forward for the job'. This approach may simply lead to the actual specification being built around someone who the interviewer 'likes'. If we only recruit people we like or 'have the right chemistry', we run the risk of not only of cloning ourselves, but also of not achieving the all-essential mix of behavioural competences in our team mix.

Next, you need to go into the business of finding candidates positively and with the clear intention of getting as many as possible to apply.

I was at a client's recently and I was talking to the Production Director, who is due to retire within a couple of years, about his plans for the recruitment of a production manager who would hopefully take over from him when he retires. I asked him whether he planned to use a full assessment centre process and his immediate response was that he would like to but that he was doubtful that they would get enough candidates. If you go into any recruitment with this attitude it can very easily become self-fulfilling.

'Sell' the job and the company to each of the candicdates

One of the things you need to do to maximise the number of candidates is to 'sell' your company and the job to each of them. You have to assume that they are currently happily employed and you therefore have to entice them to apply to work for you.

There are many things to think about here but one of them would be that if you're going to advertise the position get your **marketing** people prepare the advert - they're experts in these things - unlike the HR department or even recruitment agencies. Make sure the copy truly reflects the culture and values of the business and both the excitement and the security of working there.

Use marketing people to write the job advert

No matter what the position, you should target a minimum of four and a maximum of six people to go through some form of detailed, objective, unbiased assessment process.

At its simplest you need to assess the candidates' skills - you simply cannot rely on CVs or references.

A recent study suggested that 60% of the content of most CVs was at best overstated and at worst fabricated.

Nor can you rely on references - they often have little value in these days of concerns about possible litigation and indeed, it is not unusual for lawyers to include in a termination agreement a clause committing the former employer to providing a good reference for the former employee.So it is up to us to assess the core skills of the candidates.

Ask yourself: When we recruit a sales person do we directly establish whether they can sell?

When we recruit an accountant do we establish whether they can read, interpret and, most importantly, report on a set of accounts?

If you were to recruit a chef you'd ask him or her to prepare a meal wouldn't you?

I was recruiting a Group Finance Director for the plc I was running and as part of the recruitment process we sent a set of company monthly accounts to each of the six short-listed candidates. We gave them an instruction that when they came for the assessment centre they would be required to make a 15 minute presentation on the state of the company, the areas of concern and their recommendations for both immediate and longer-term actions – just from their interpretation of the figures.

Interestingly, the person we finally recruited later told me that in his entire career he had never been asked to do this before at an interview, that he found it

Set up a realistic way to assess candidate's core skills

extremely testing and that he considered that it was most definitely the right thing to do when recruiting.

It is my view that the assessment process is so critical that it's worth putting a great deal of effort into getting it right. I would therefore always try and put in place a full one-day assessment centre, involving all short listed candidates (generally between four and six). This should be run by a facilitator and incorporate group and individual activities including, as a second level differentiator only, verbal, numerical and diagrammatic reasoning and a psychometric analysis.

Use assessment centres to evaluate candidates

I have been an assessor now at, probably, close to a hundred assessment centres seeking to select candidates for positions from shop floor supervisors, new graduates right through to CEOs and presidents across four continents. My guess would be that in well over half of the cases the candidate who we all felt we would have selected prior to the assessment centre was not the candidate who came through at the end as the right person for the job.

The final stage in the recruitment process should be a face-to-face discussion and negotiation between the selected

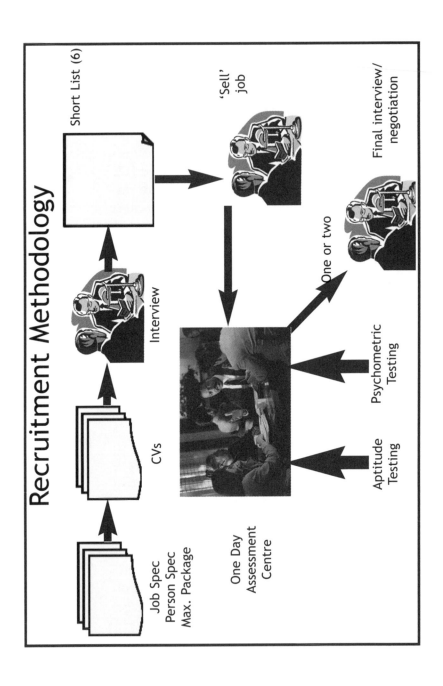

Recruitment Methodology

Job Spec
Person Spec
Max. Package

CVs

Interview

Short List (6)

'Sell' job

One Day Assessment Centre

Aptitude Testing

Psychometric Testing

One or two

Final interview/negotiation

candidate and his or her 'boss to be' and finally I would always recommend a period of probation before the job is finally confirmed.

My plea to all CEOs and business leaders is, therefore, to get in your helicopter and ask yourself the question :

Can there be anything more important to the sustained profitable growth of your business than recruiting right?

And if there isn't then please listen to your HR people and invest enough of your time and finance to ensure that you seek to recruit right every time!

My full 'Recruit to Win', recruiting methodology is available in either eBook or CD format on my website, www.rogerharrop.com

It simply will improve your profitability!

Three Dimensional Leadership

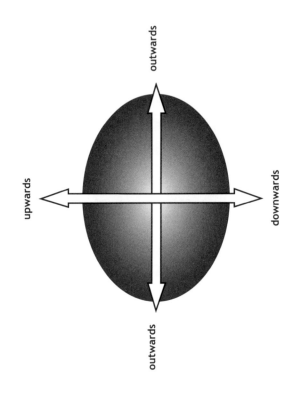

Leadership

Many things have been written and said about leadership, but looking down from my helicopter it is clear to me that the successful leader needs to exhibit three attributes above all others:

Belief
Passion
Courage

We discussed earlier in this book the need for a clear business purpose – you need to truly believe in that purpose, and that you will achieve it 100%. Any less and people will see through you.

You need to exhibit a real passion for the business and its responsibilities and values for people to follow you and finally you will not succeed without being courageous – to take risks – and make the really difficult decisions.

Remember people will follow what you do, not what you say

As leaders you also need to recognise the essential three dimensions of leadership (see illustration on page 52).

Upwards leadership is the one most often forgotten - and probably the most difficult. It is about taking your courage in your hands and telling those above you what they need to hear rather than what they may want to hear. And by the way ...

Do I make it easy for my people to tell me what I need to hear?

How easy do you make it for those below you to tell you what you need to hear?

Staying in the Helicopter

54

The Change House

This model (see page 56) was developed by Professor Paul Kirkbride and proposes that any organisation, be it a company, department, team, or indeed individual, exists at any time in one of four 'rooms' and furthermore can only move from room to room in a predetermined sequence.

The leadership needs of the business, and the people in it, are different for each room and I believe you will find this model a particularly valuable tool in your armoury.

Room of Contentment

Here you will find organisations, teams and groups that may have been highly successful – and maybe still are – but have allowed themselves the luxury of thinking that they know it all, that if they carry on the way they always have that they will be, and indeed are entitled to be, continually successful.

'Problems, what problems?' they will say as they pat each other on the back, hold expensive sales conferences, get less cost conscious and publish the history of the company!

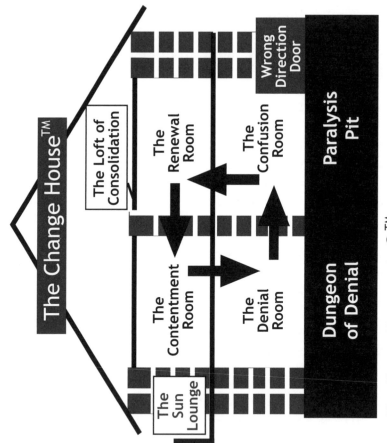

The Change House™

The Change House Model© ™

The Loft of Consolidation

The Renewal Room

The Confusion Room

Paralysis Pit

Wrong Direction Door

The Contentment Room

The Denial Room

Dungeon of Denial

The Sun Lounge

Some may become so complacent they take their eyes right off the ball and go out on the sun lounger whilst telling all that 'We are the best' and 'Nothing can stop us'. The immediate signs to look for include designated car parking, lots of internal publications and inbreeding!

I can think of a number of major corporations in the recent past that were firmly located in this room – and at least one political party!

There is only one place to go from here.

Room of Denial

You'll find a lot of finger pointing in this room - any problems are 'transient' or 'someone else's fault'. There's a focus on looking to past achievements whilst people become irrationally optimistic and search for comforting data - and of course, statements are made like 'Our business is different'.

This is the most dangerous room of all to be in because unless a catalyst for realism and change appears then the Dungeon of Denial beckons! The catalyst is often a new CEO, or external influencer who sets a very clear, simple, believable, achievable goal and repeats it endlessly whilst injecting

Do I recognise which room we are in currently?

armfuls of realism into the organisation to pull and push them into the next room.

Room of Confusion

This is where the journey can be very uncomfortable. There are 'so many problems'.

There is lots of activity, lots of half-finished initiatives, consultants everywhere and revolving doors for people coming and going. People are desperate for direction - speculation and rumours abound.

To survive this room and move forward it is vital that the CEO continues to repeat the simple message and goal set in the Room of Denial – so a light can be seen at end of the tunnel. If not, there is a risk of the organisation sinking into the paralysis pit as people say 'I'm confused, I don't understand – I think the safest thing is for me to keep my head down'.

Another danger here is the Wrong Direction Door. It can be very uncomfortable in this room and relief can sometimes be seen by dashing off in an ill-thought-out direction which solves nothing. How many times, for example, do we see company boards deciding that an acquisition is the answer – and the result?

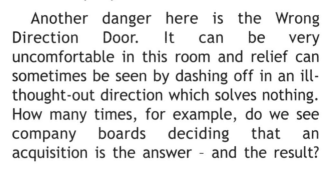

Have we gone through the Wrong Direction Door?

Staying in the Helicopter

Two non-performing companies rather than one!

Room of Renewal

This is the room you strive be in – and it is a remarkable and rewarding place to be. Here you find everyone singing from the same hymn sheet, taking ownership and working together. Where problems are seen as 'ours', progress is measured and new targets are set. Whilst success is celebrated, the paradigms are constantly under challenge and the bar is always being raised.

This is where you want to be – and to stay!

But it's much harder than you may think – that Room of Contentment is very alluring! Look at Manchester United who were an outstanding example of an organisation who managed to keep in the Renewal Room for season after season until they finally allowed themselves to slip into that very attractive Room of Contentment the year that the manager said he was retiring.

How do I get my business into and then stay in the Room of Renewal?

The Change House

59

PROFITABLE GROWTH MATRIX™

£m	Last Full Year Result	Regain and Retain Lost Customers	Increase Order Value and Frequency	Price	'Helicopter' Sales and Marketing	Belbin Selected Teams	Next Full Year Forecast
Sales	10	1.5	1.3	0.4	0.3	0.5	14.0
Operating Profit	1	0.15	0.13	0.4	0.13	0.05	1.86
Return on Sales	10%						13%

Profitable Growth Matrix™

People may say that it's all very well talking about these initiatives to achieve profitable growth – but can we 'walk the talk' and translate them into real numbers?

Each time I run a Helicopter workshop or masterclass I ask the delegates to complete a Profitable Growth Matrix™ with their considered, ideally conservative, view of what they believe is achievable in a typical company for the next full year financial results. Over 2000 CEOs, have gone through the programme and the PGM on page 60, completed by a group of twelve delegates – all experienced CEOs, is absolutely typical of what CEOs believe they could achieve using the secrets and tools we have shared.

A 40% increase in sales and an 86% increase in profits!!

Can you afford to ignore profitable growth like this?

Over 2000 CEOs can't be wrong!

Set my profitable growth target - now!

Profitable Growth Matrix

61

CEOs' Helicopter Checklist

 Do I get in the helicopter often enough?

 Is our overriding business purpose crystal clear?

 Discipline of market leaders

- *What does the heartbeat of my organisation say about where the focus and energy is?*

- *Have we made a clear choice?*

- *Are we targeting customer groups who value this?*

- *Is the organisation aligned with the strategy?*

- *Are we always looking to move the benchmarks upwards?*

Do we have mechanisms in place to generate ideas for 'new sandboxes'?

 Do I get the right Key Performance information at the right time and in the right financial language?

 Do we have a profitable growth strategy that builds on existing customers first?

 Do I need to look at prices?

 Do we have an adequate mix of Belbin team profiles in each of our teams?

 Am I clear exactly how we are addressing each stage in the Universal Buying Process?

 Do I use the best methods to recruit?

 How do I get my business into, and then stay in, the Room of Renewal?

 Complete My Profitable Growth Matrix™

CEOs' Helicopter Checklist

MY PROFITABLE GROWTH MATRIX™

	Last Full Year Result	Regain and Retain Lost Customers	Increase Order Value and Frequency	Price	'Helicopter' Sales and Marketing	Belbin Selected Teams	Next Full Year Forecast
Sales							
Operating Profit							
Return on Sales							

My Profitable Growth Matrix™

Have a look at your business from the helicopter and see what you believe you can achieve.

Now just go out and make it happen!

NO! DON'T JUST PUT THIS BOOK ON THE SHELF!

I know you haven't any time. I know your heart says you should do something, but your head says you're too busy.

Remember - if you want to eat an elephant you have to slice it up!

Set yourself a realistic programme now – promise yourself to get in your helicopter at least once a month (maybe put the next six occasions in your diary) and address a section of this book each time and put specific actions in place. (And whilst you are at it why not delegate more? - go on try it!)

Good luck and enjoy!

Biography

Roger Harrop BSc(Hons)., CEng., FIMechE., FCIM., FInstIB., MPSA.

Roger is an international speaker, non-executive director, business advisor, mentor, author and consultant focused on improved sustained profitable growth.

He has extensive experience across a broad spectrum of businesses - from small start-ups to large multinational corporations; from high tech manufactured products through basic commodities, to people based services businesses.

Roger spent seven years as Group Chief Executive of a fully quoted, high-tech industrial instrumentation group with 12 operations over three continents. The company was listed in the UK Government's 'Competitiveness' white paper and gained a reference in the US *Forbes* magazine as one of the top 100 'small' overseas companies and has been used as a benchmark case study by two business schools on culture change and business re-engineering. He has run businesses for major multinational companies and has been a tutor with one of the leading leadership and teambuilding programmes for over 20 years.

Roger is a member of the Professional Speakers Association. a former Vice-President of the Institution of Mechanical Engineers, and a Liveryman with the Worshipful Company of Marketors.

He is an accredited SME business advisor, a trained assessor and coach, and is on the chairman panel with a number of private equity houses.

To book Roger Harrop for a keynote, seminar, workshop, master class, strategic planning event or to discuss consultancy advice email roger@rogerharrop.com

Bibliography

Seven Habits Of Highly Effective People by Stephen R. Covey. Published by Free Press; ISBN: 0 6717086 3 5

The Discipline of Market Leaders: Choose Your Customers, Narrow Your Focus, Dominate Your Market by Michael Treacy & Fred Wiersema. Published by Perseus Books; ASIN: 0 2014064 8 9

Strategy Pure & Simple II: How Winning Companies Dominate Their Competitors by Michel Robert. Published by McGraw-Hill; ISBN: 0 0705313 3 1

How to Win Customers and Keep Them for Life by Michael LeBoeuf. Published by Berkeley Books; ISBN: 0 4251750 1 4

The viral marketing clip and statistics are shown with permission from The Viral Factory (www.theviralfactory.com)

Belbin team roles are reproduced with permission from Belbin Associates (www.belbin.com)

The Change House Model©™ is used with permission of The Change House Limited (www.thechangehouse.com)

Staying in the Helicopter